I0493726

Hydra: 40 Drawings

BY ERIK VATNE

Poetry

CXX Epistles (forthcoming)
Pulaski Skyway & Other Poems (forthcoming 2013)
The Mt. Sinai Poems
X Sonnets (forthcoming)
Words in Search of a Meaning
Mormon Heroin
Dun Scotus on His Sickbed
XXIII Epistles
Cartographies of Silence
Endings

Visual/Performance

The Lovers (2012) 5 minutes, from series of 23 short films

Cartographies of Silence: performance/reading with music by Cliff Thompson (You Tube) at Bowery Poetry Club, August, 2010

Hydra: 40 Drawings

Psychopathia Sexualis (paintings)

32 Italian Verbs: Works-on-Paper (forthcoming)

The S.B. Notebooks: Volumes I-XX (forthcoming)
(visual phenomena)

GARAGE: Photographies (forthcoming)

Crossing the Saugatuck: Drawings, Photographies & Poems
(forthcoming)

Hydra: 40 Drawings

Erik Vatne

BURNING
APPLE
PRESS

Copyright 2013 Erik Vatne

All rights reserved. Except for short passages for purposes of review, no part of this book may be reproduced in any form or by any means, electronic or mechanical, including photocopying, recording, or by any information storage and retrieval system, without permission from the publisher.

Published by Burning Apple Press
110 Chestnut Ridge Road
#166
Montvale, NJ 07645
E-mail: burningapplepress@hotmail.com

Design: Liza Littlefield
Front cover: "Untitled 11" by Erik Vatne
Typeset: Liza Littlefield
        lizalittlefield.com, liza.littlefield@yahoo.com
Back cover photo: Self-Portrait, 2012

Hydra: 40 Drawings was composed in July 2013 and is part of a larger multi-media work of drawings, works-on-paper, photographs and poems called *Crossing the Saugatuck* to be published in 2014. Drawings 3.5" x 5.5," charcoal on paper.

Thanks: Liza, Dylan, and family & friends

        Library of Congress Cataloging-in-Publication Data

Vatne, Erik
ISBN: 0615913067

Manufactured in the United States of America

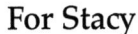

For Stacy

Hydra: 40 Drawings

CONTENTS

Untitled #22

Untitled #23

Untitled #24

Untitled #25

Untitled #26

Untitled #27

Untitled #28

Untitled #29

Untitled #30

Untitled #31

Untitled #32

Untitled #33

Untitled #34

Untitled #35

Untitled #36

Untitled #37

Untitled #38

Untitled #39

Untitled #40

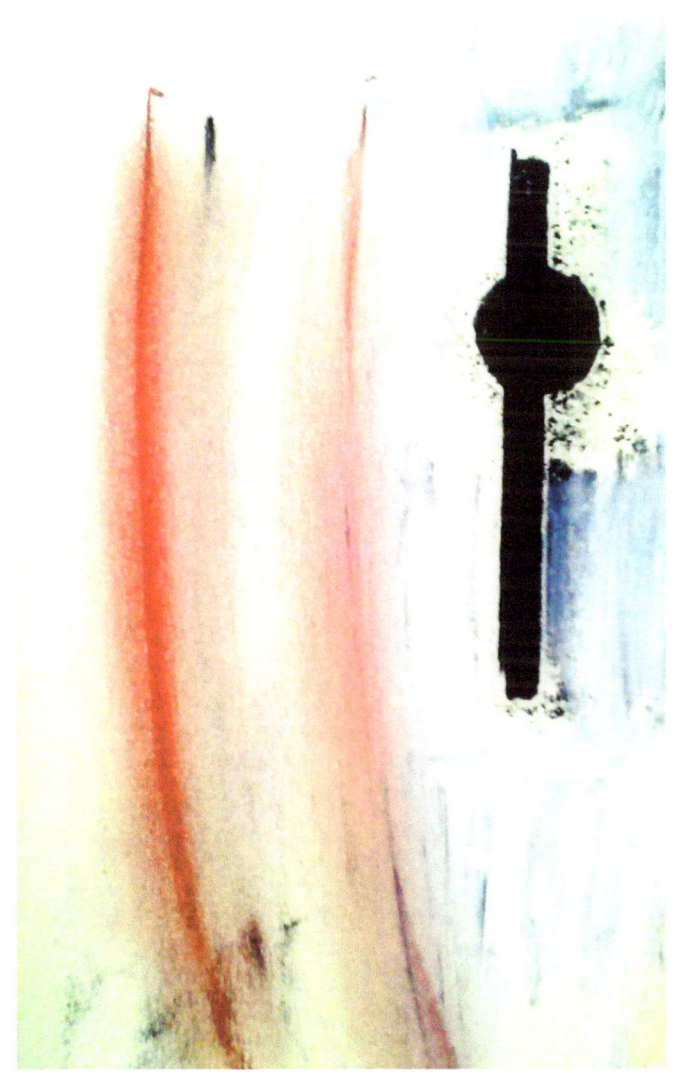

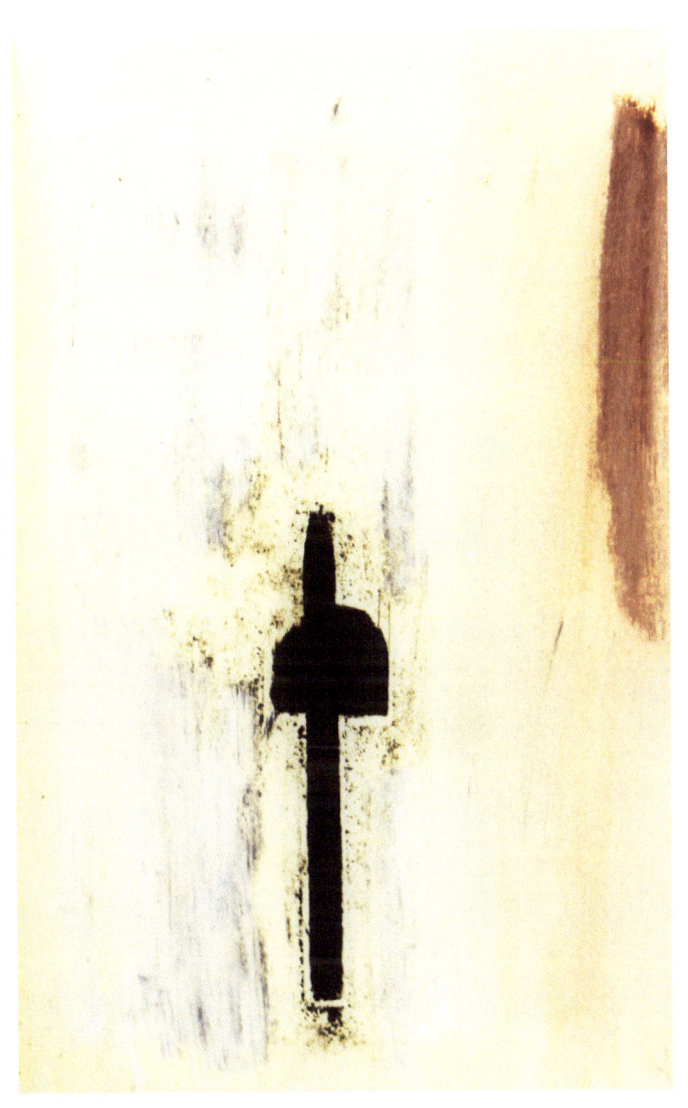

3

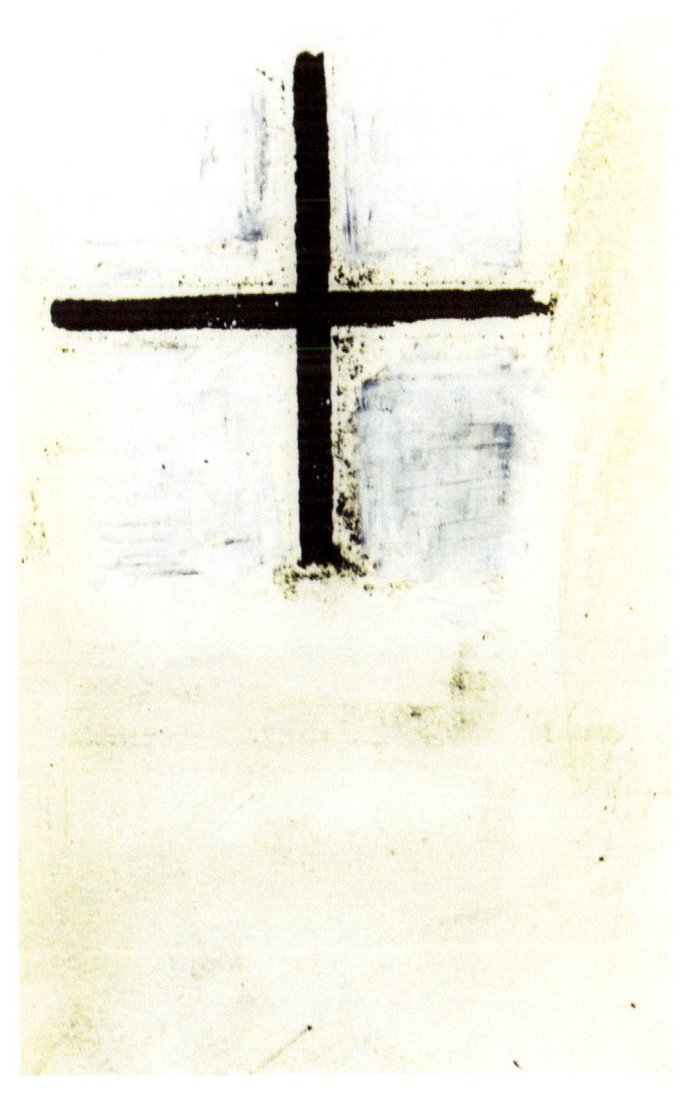

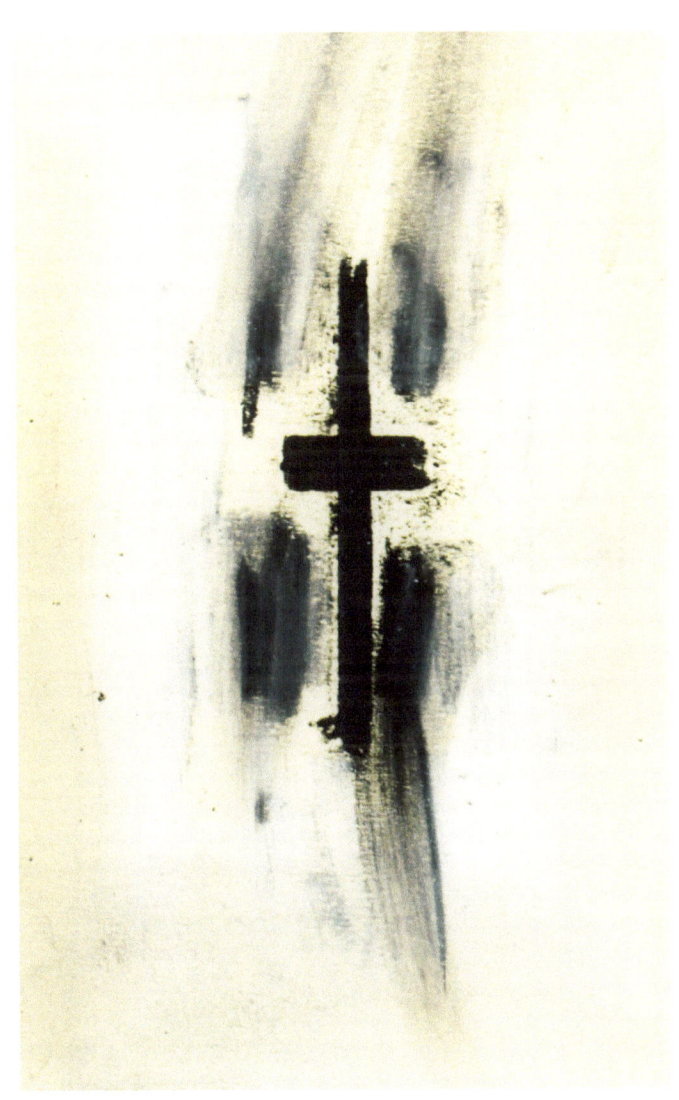

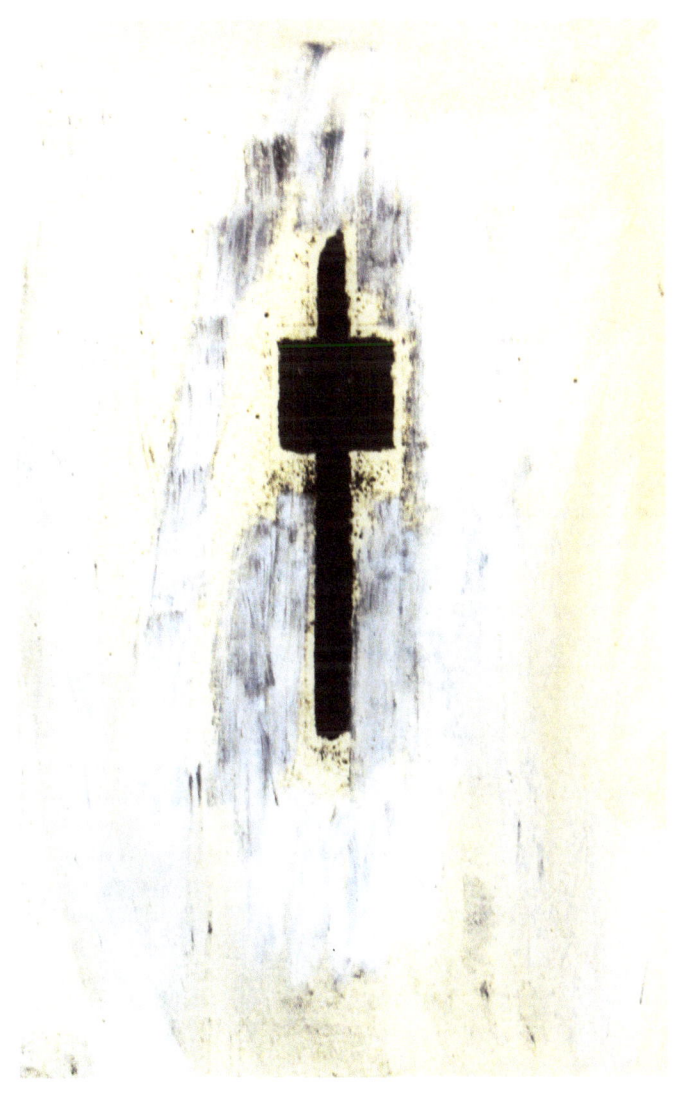

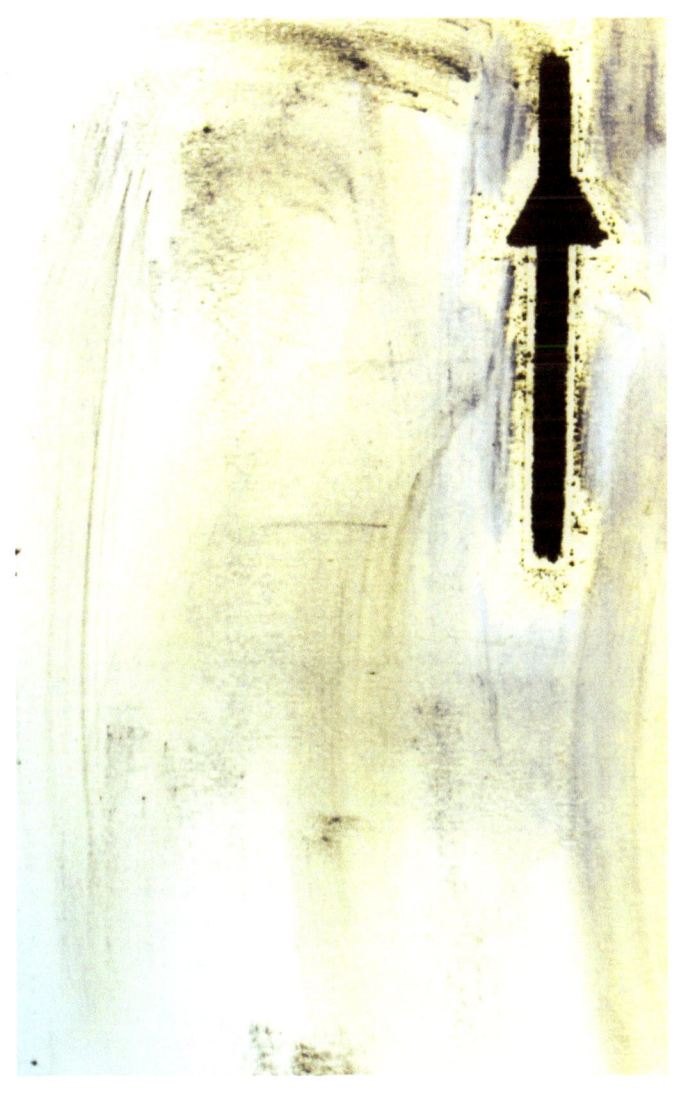

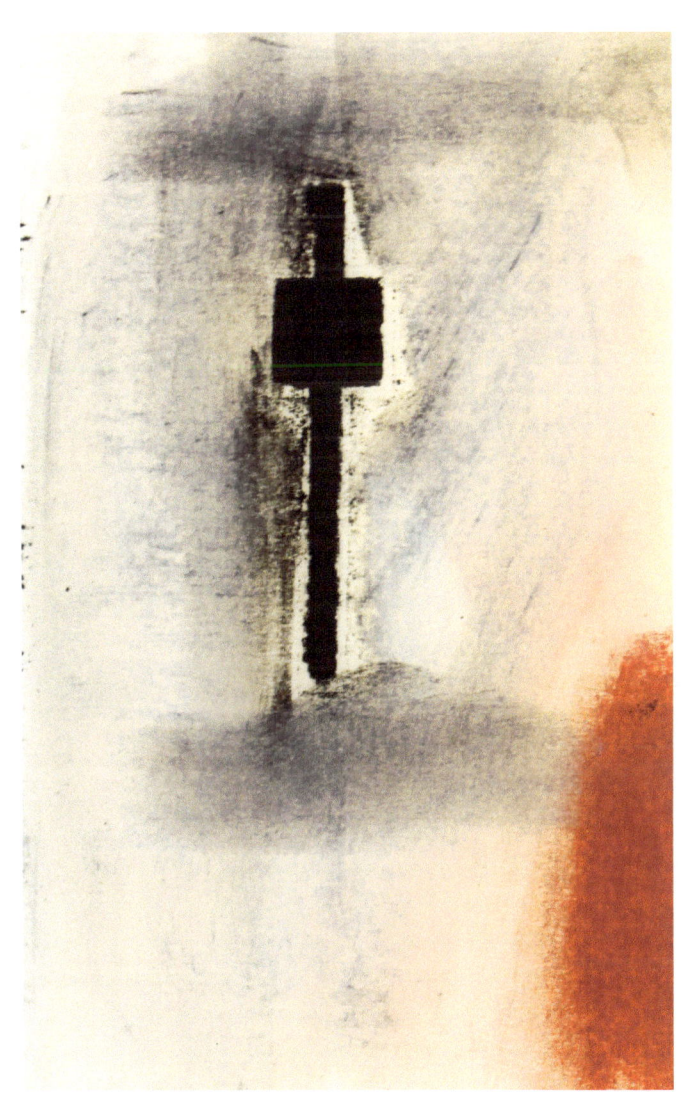

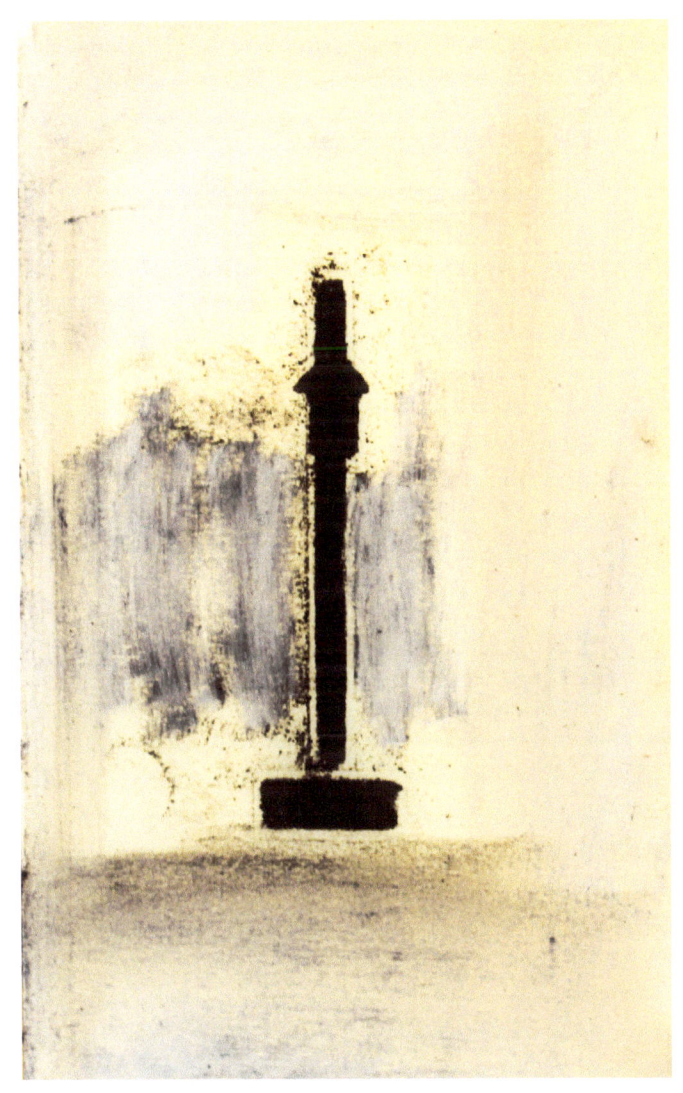

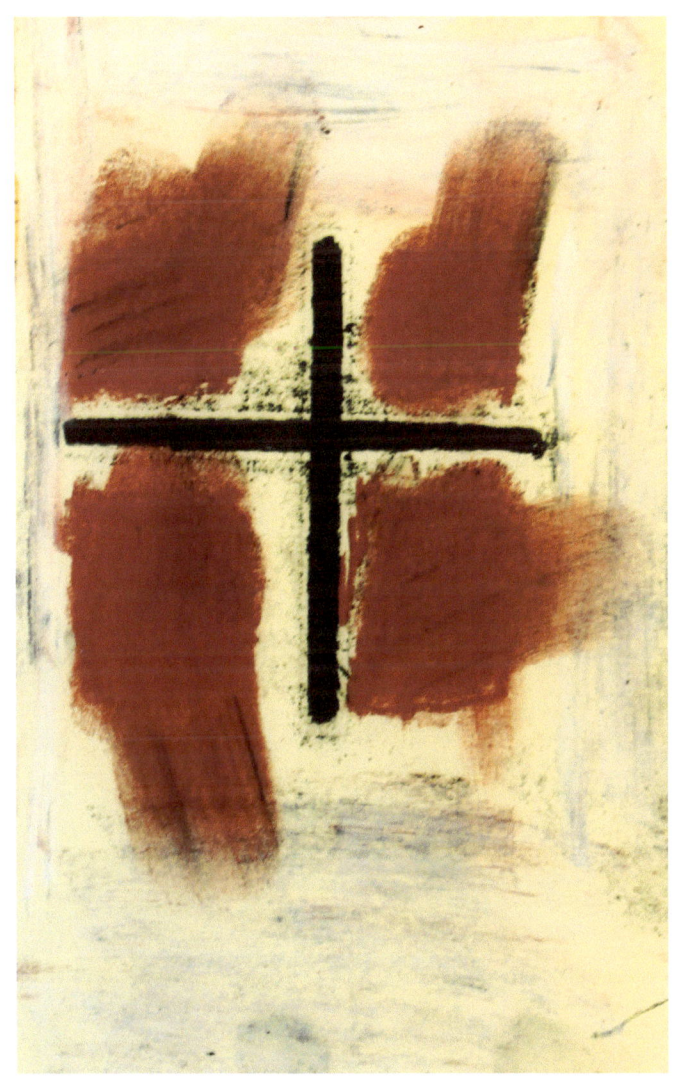

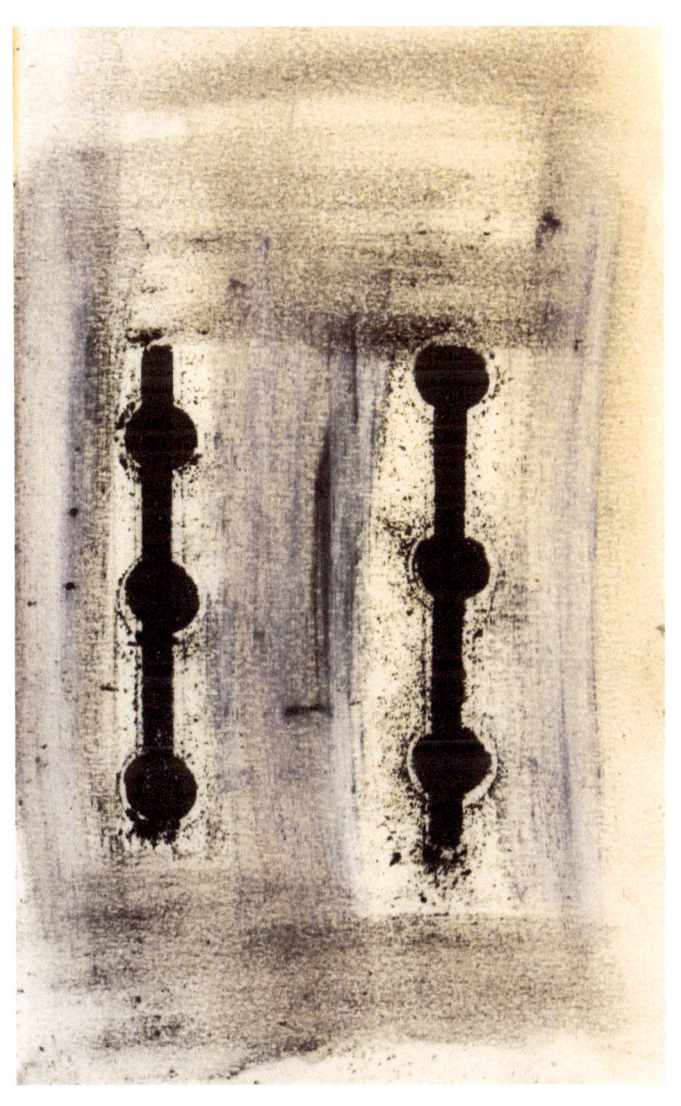

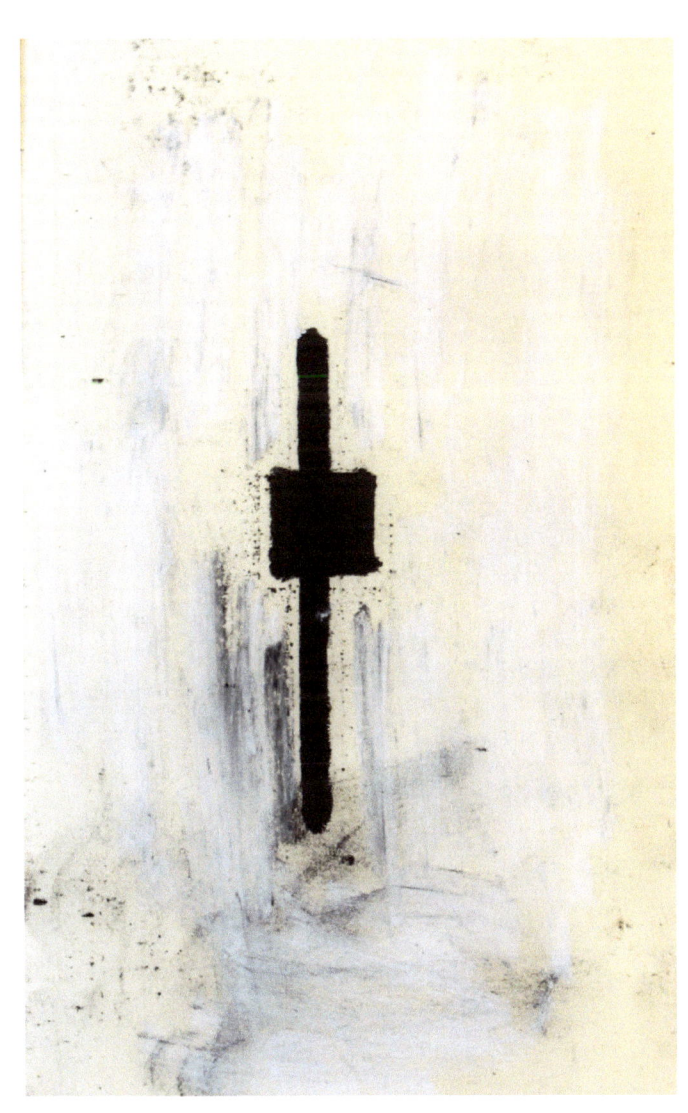

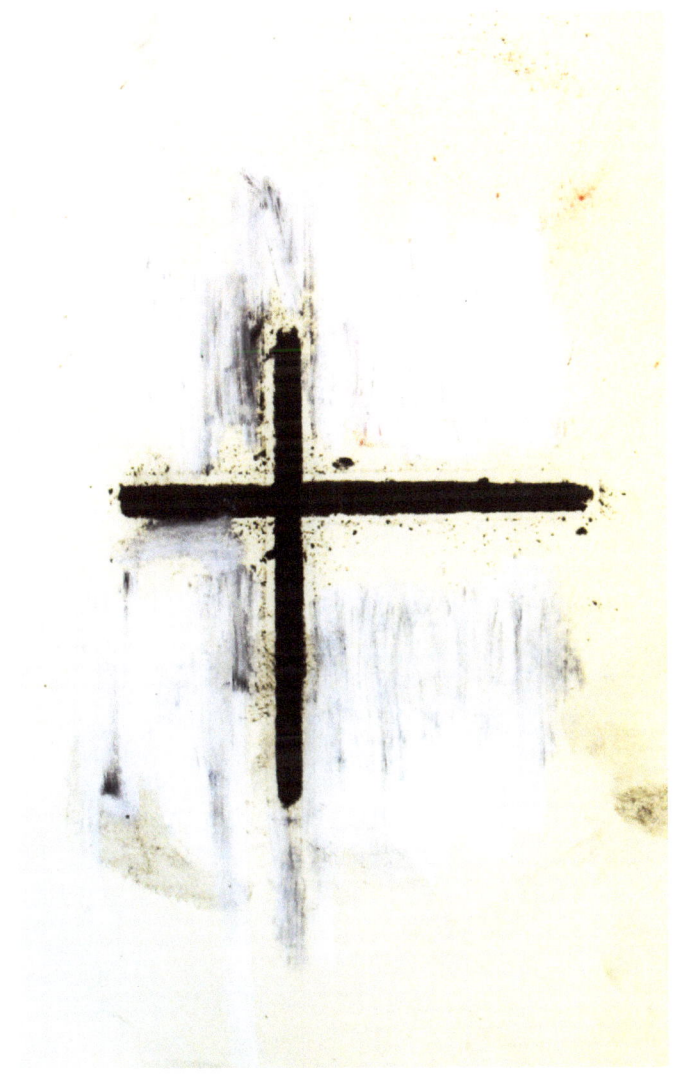

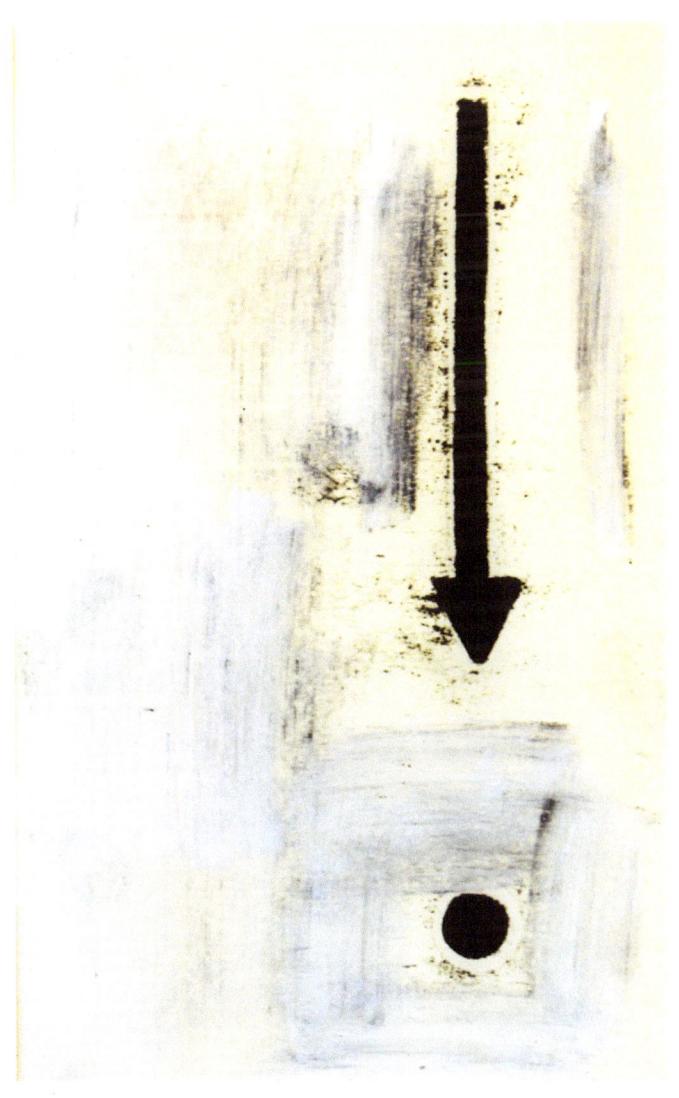

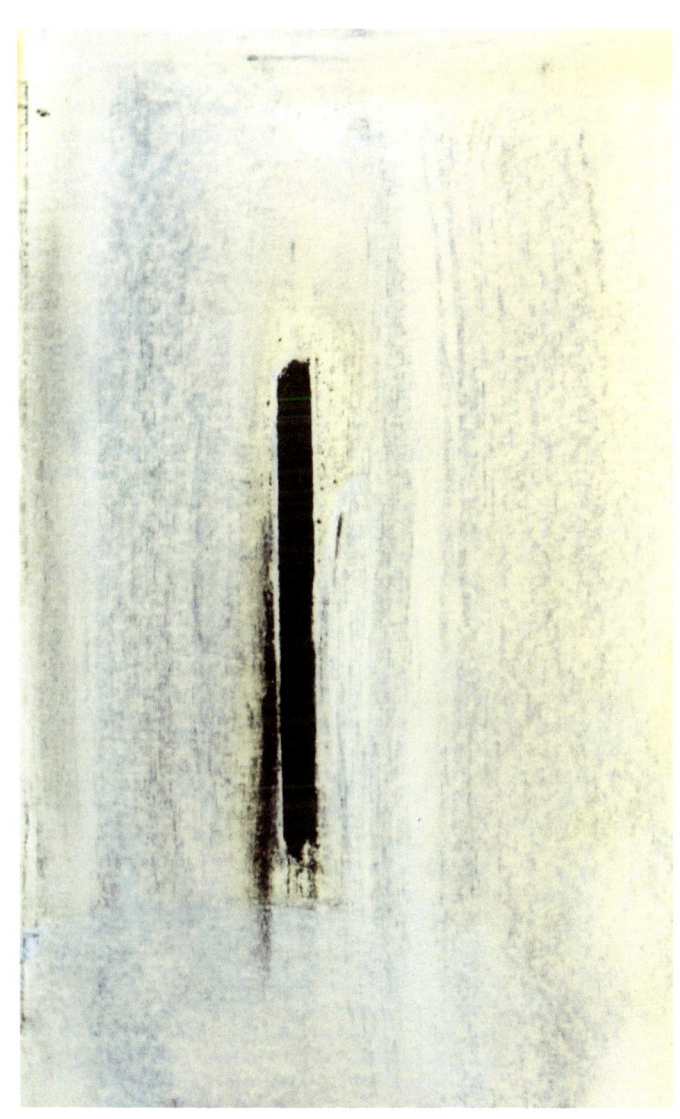

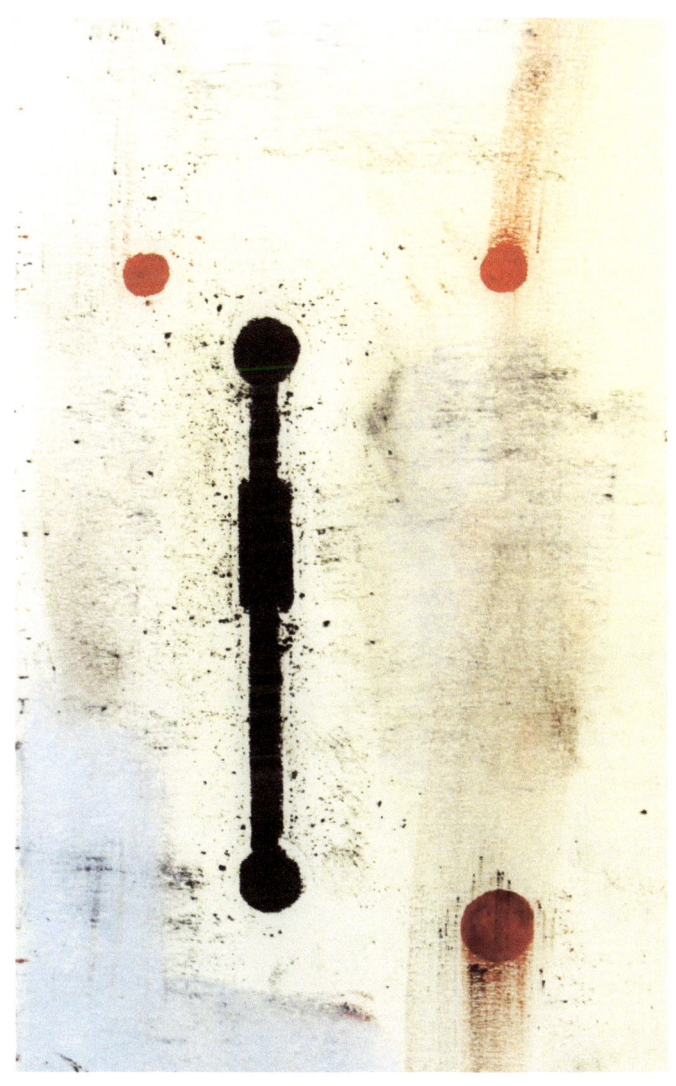

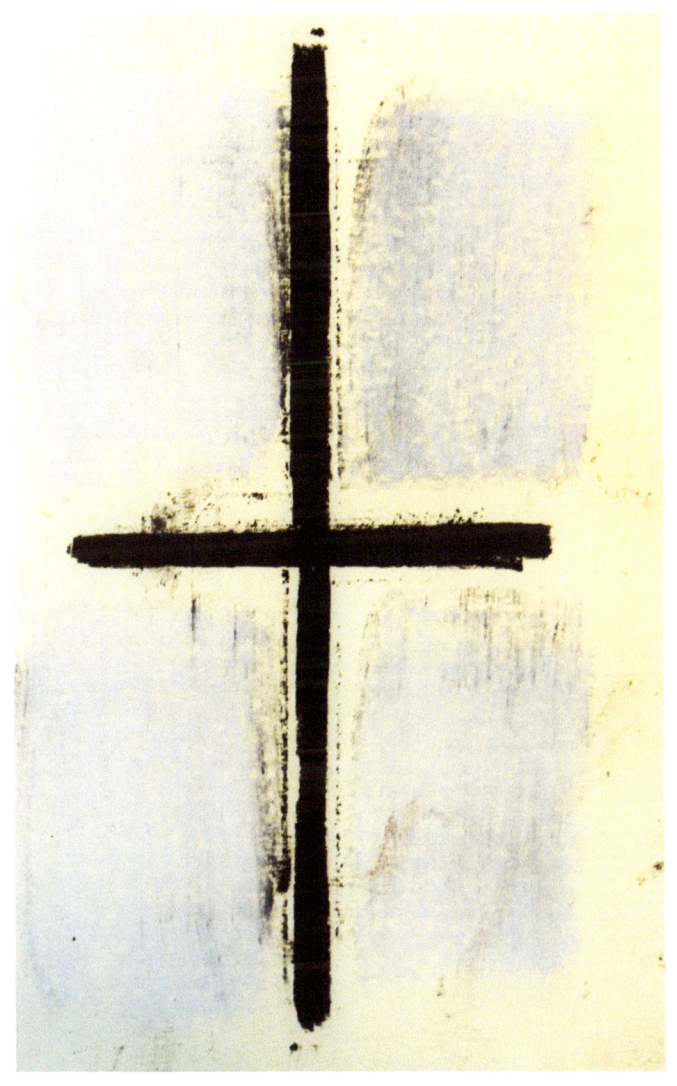

18

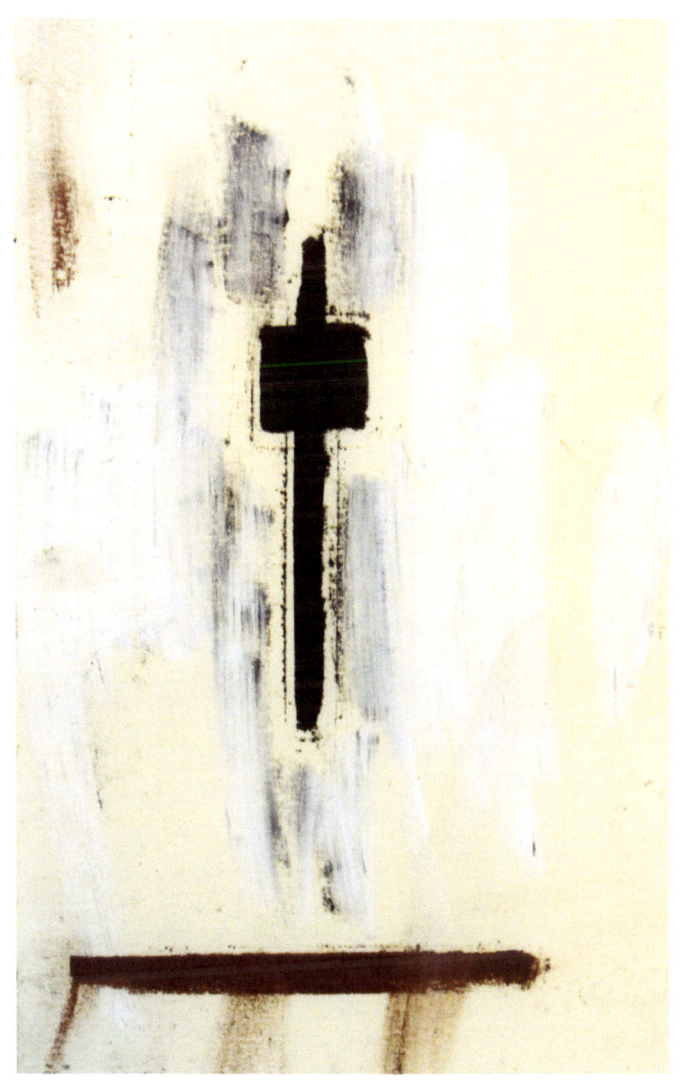

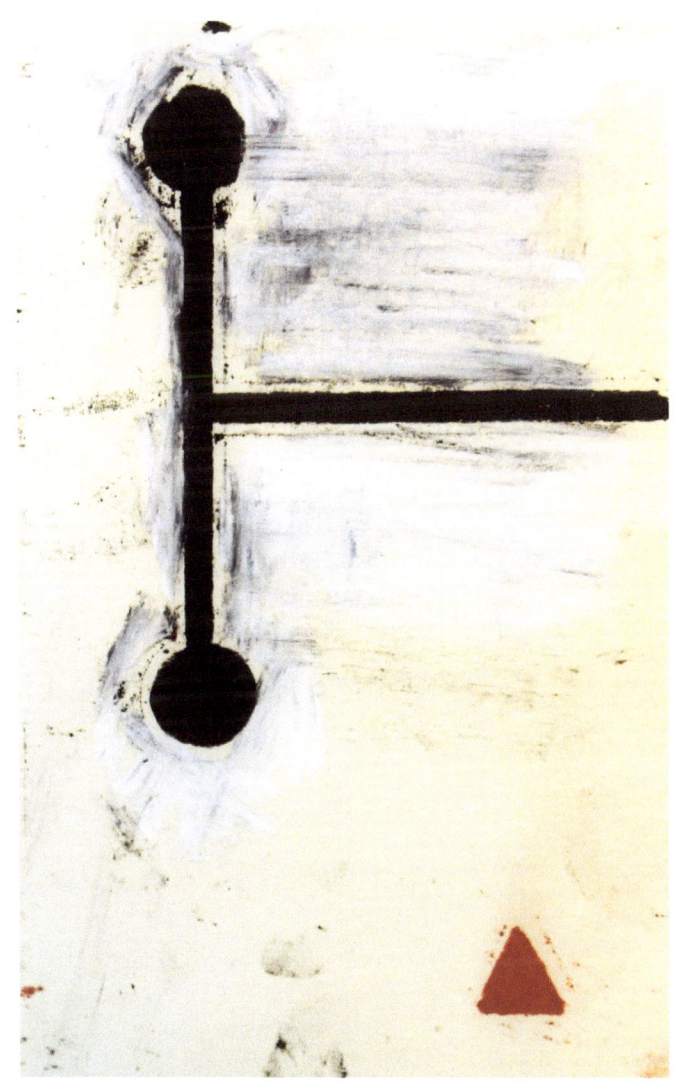

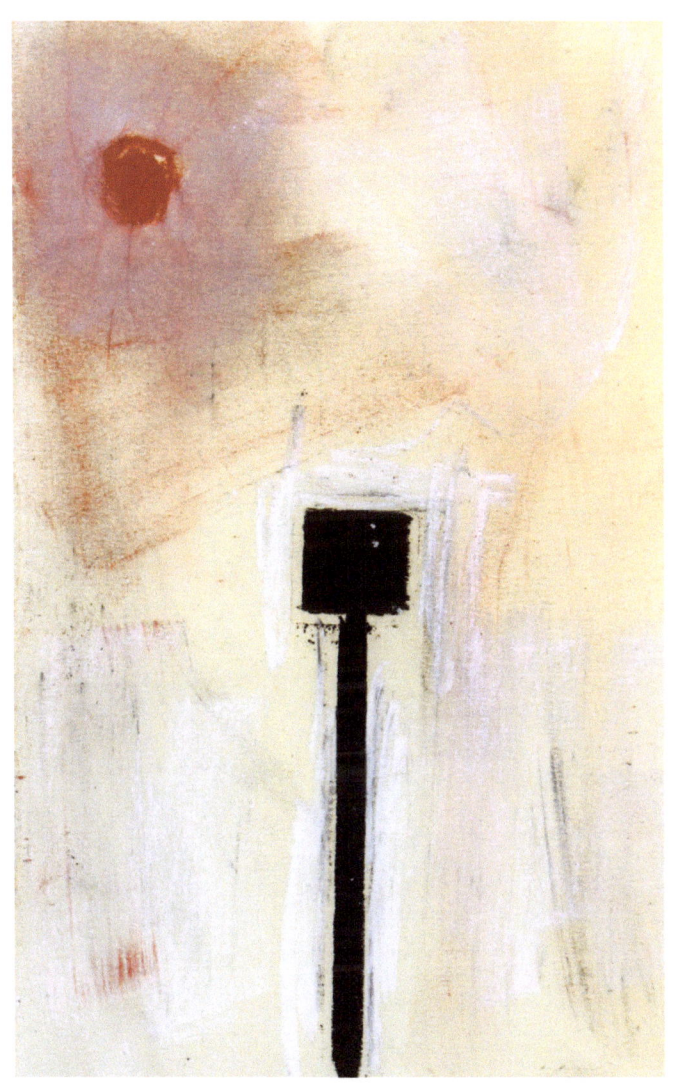

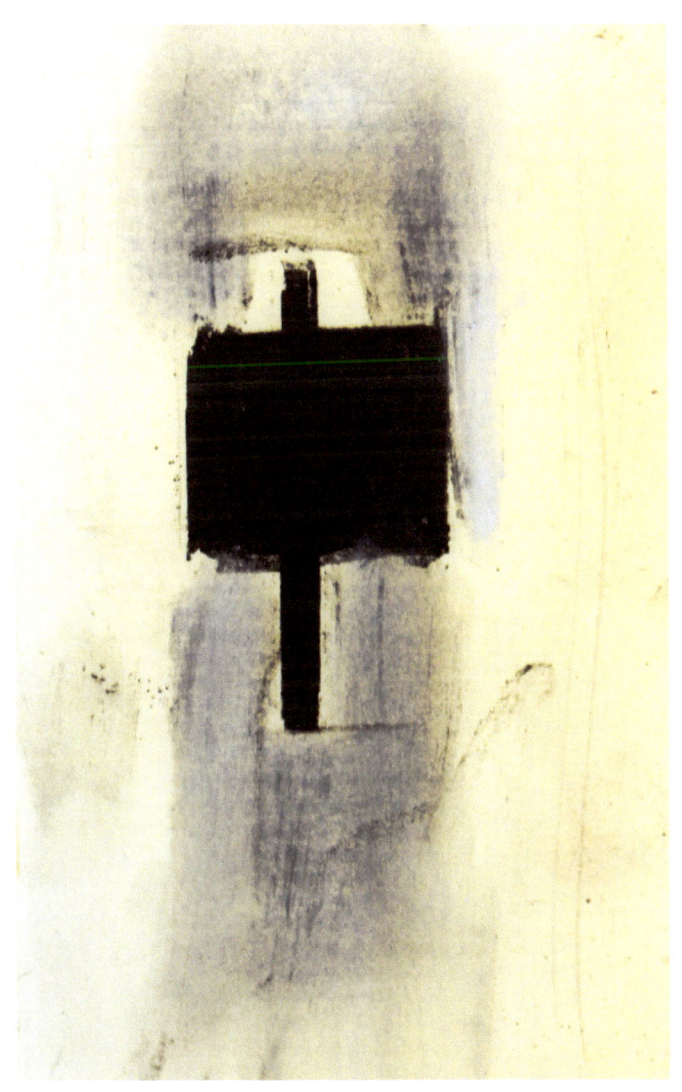

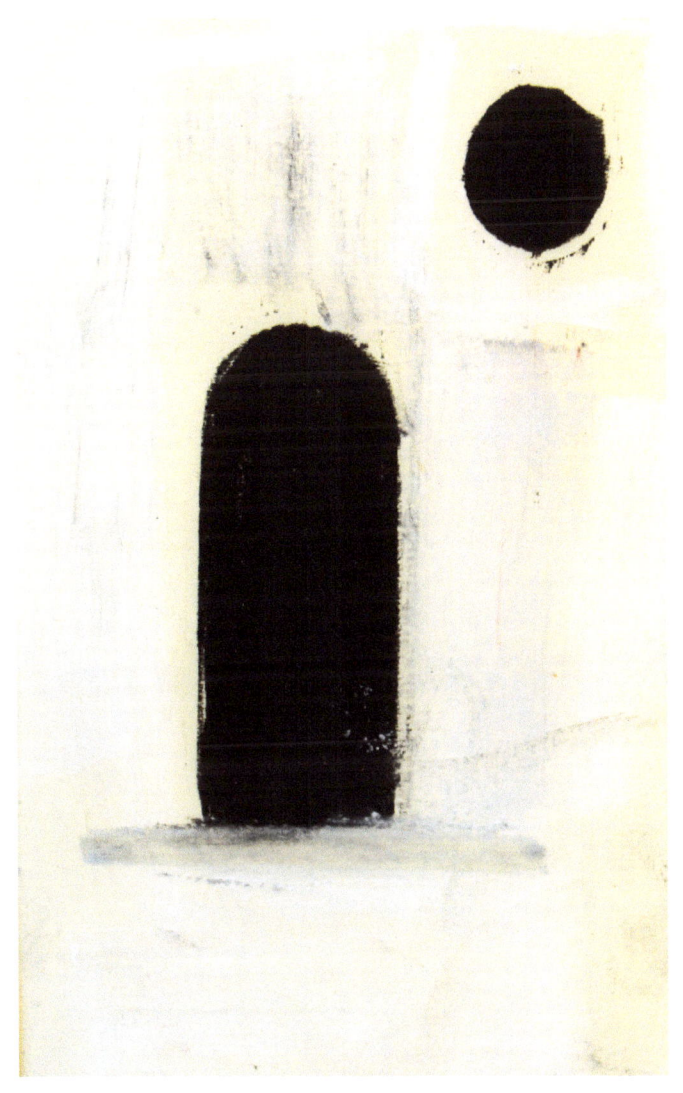

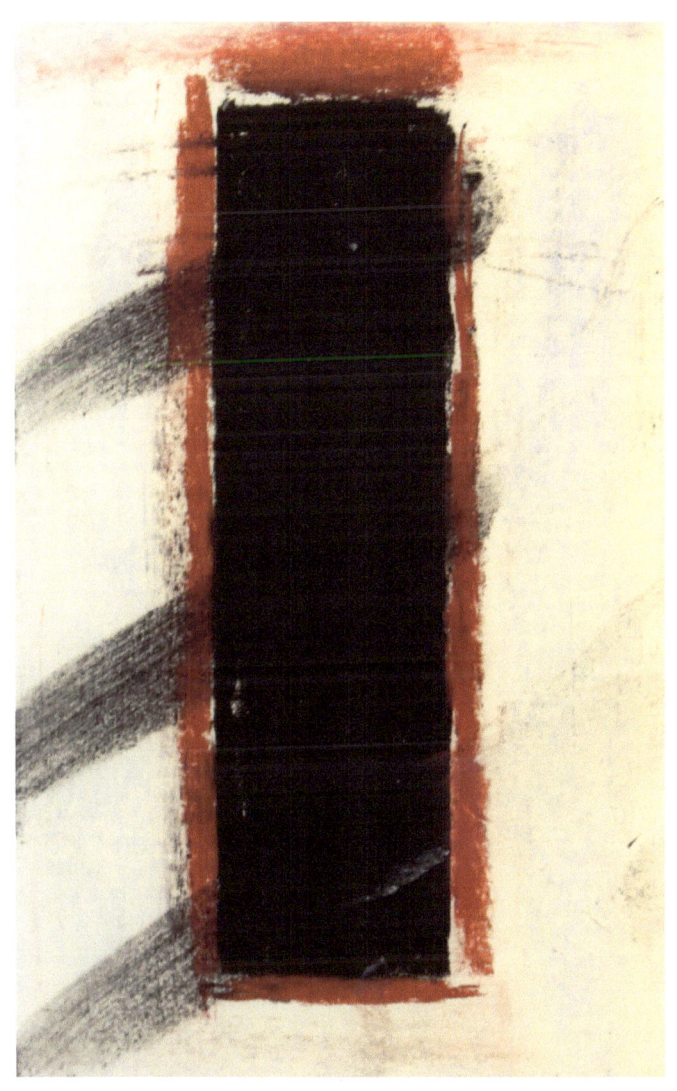

24

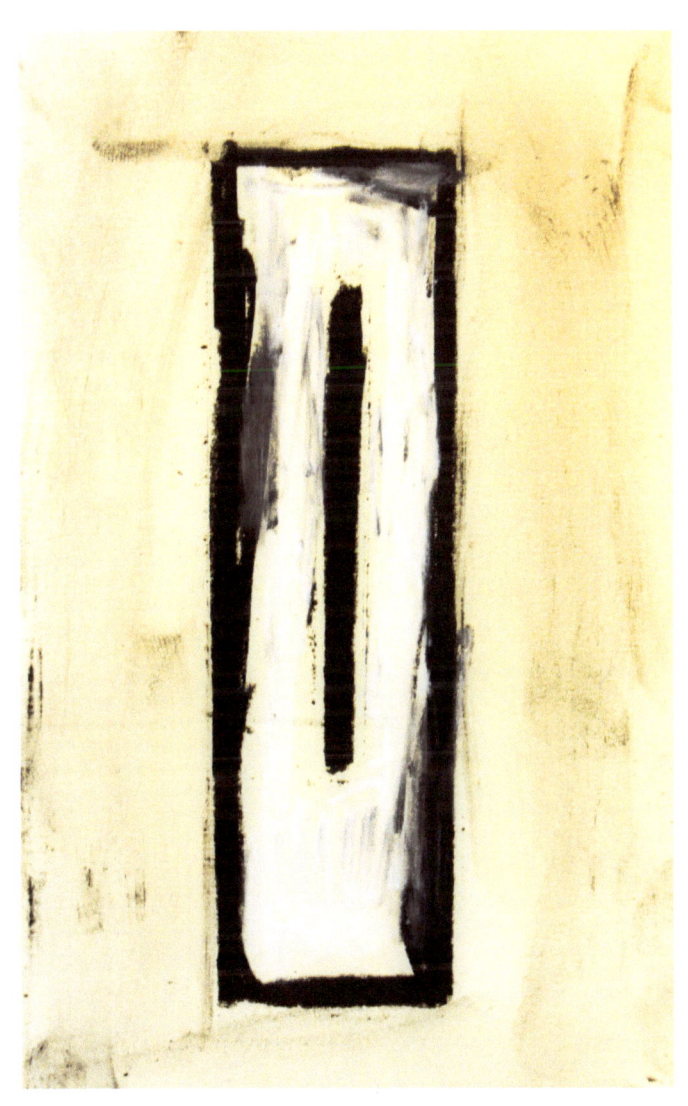

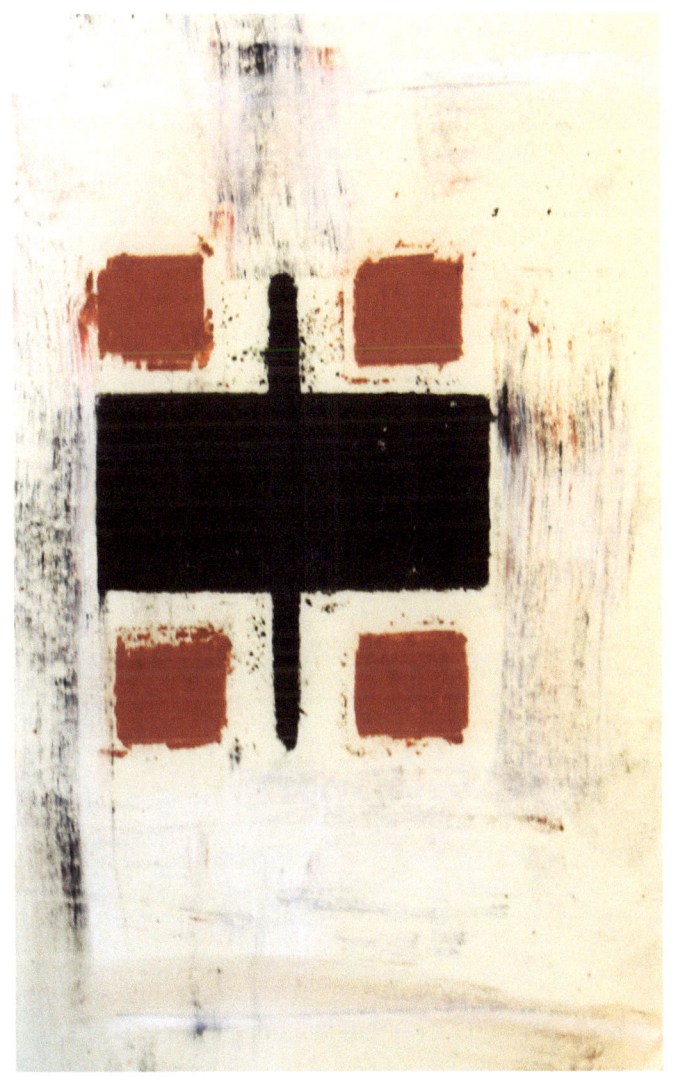

26

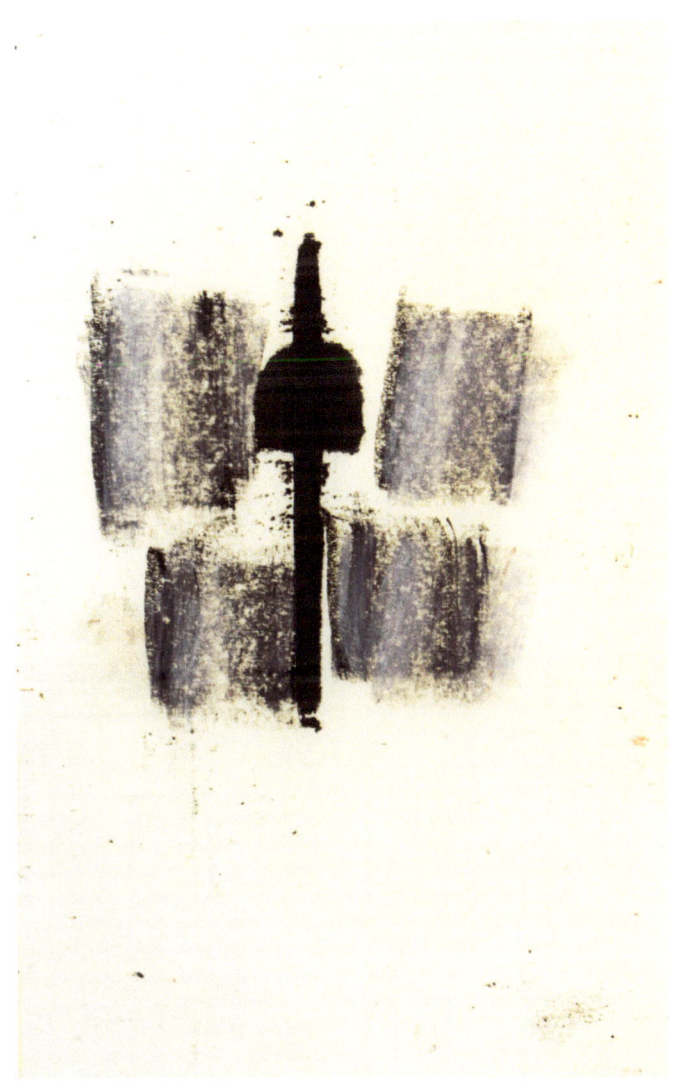

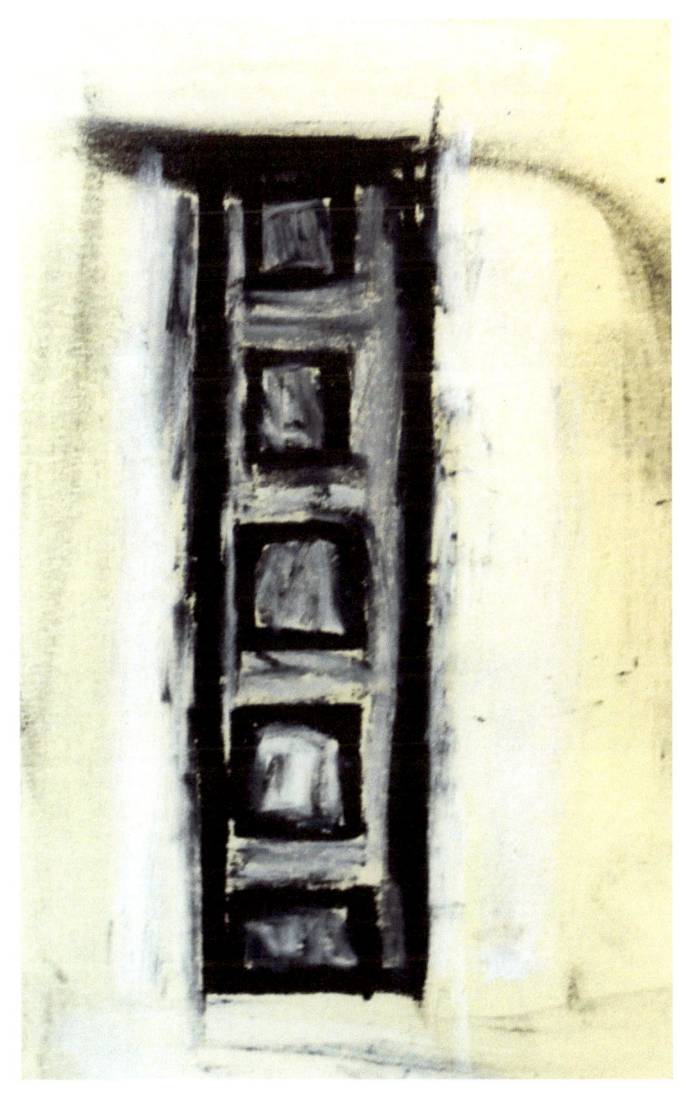

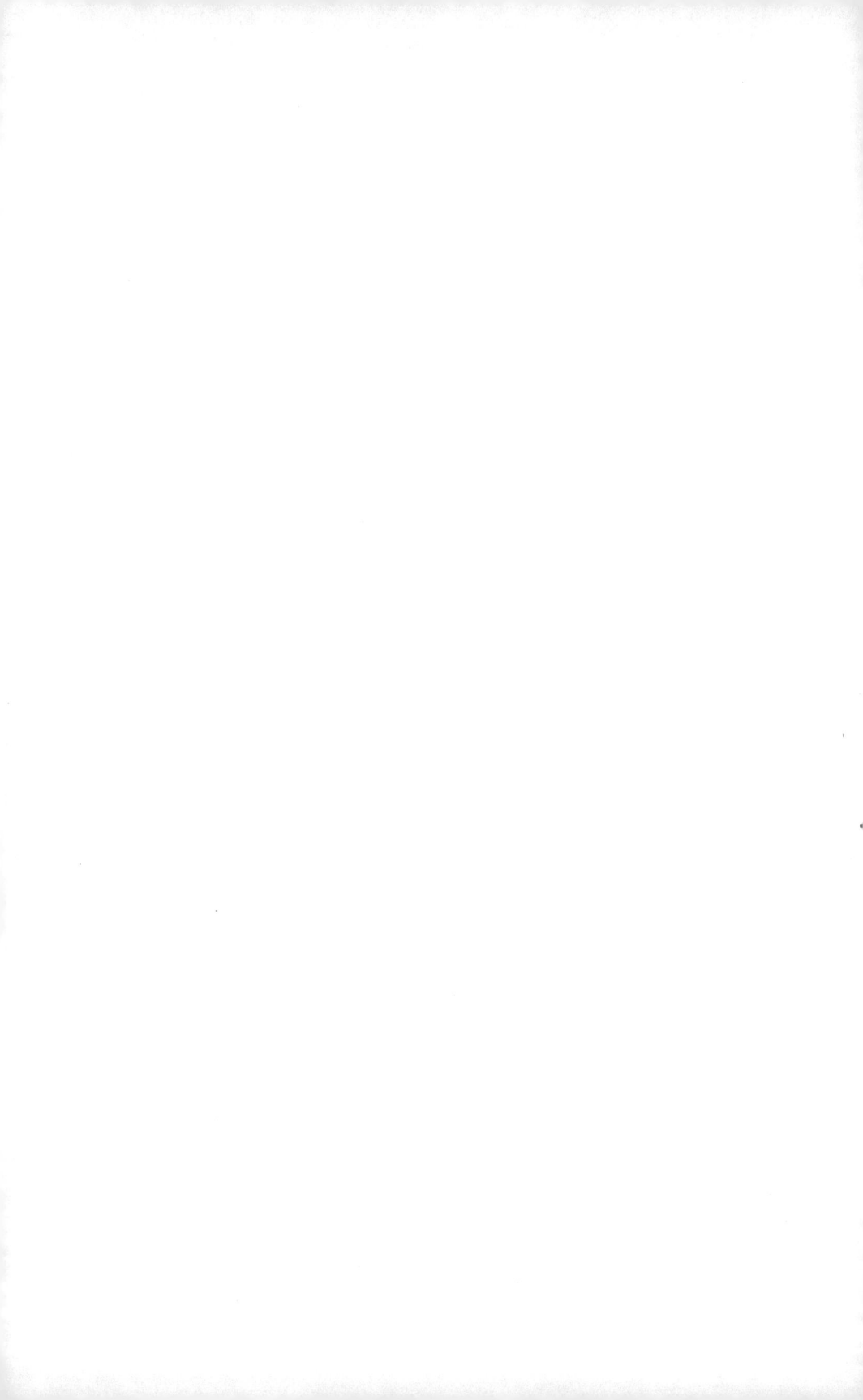

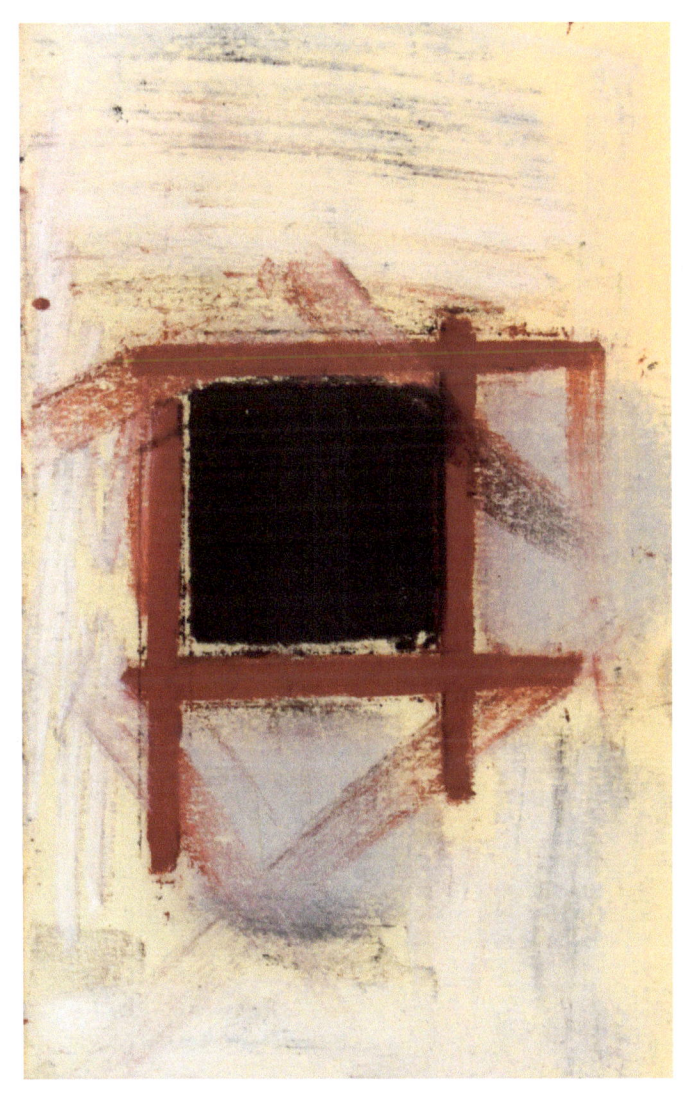

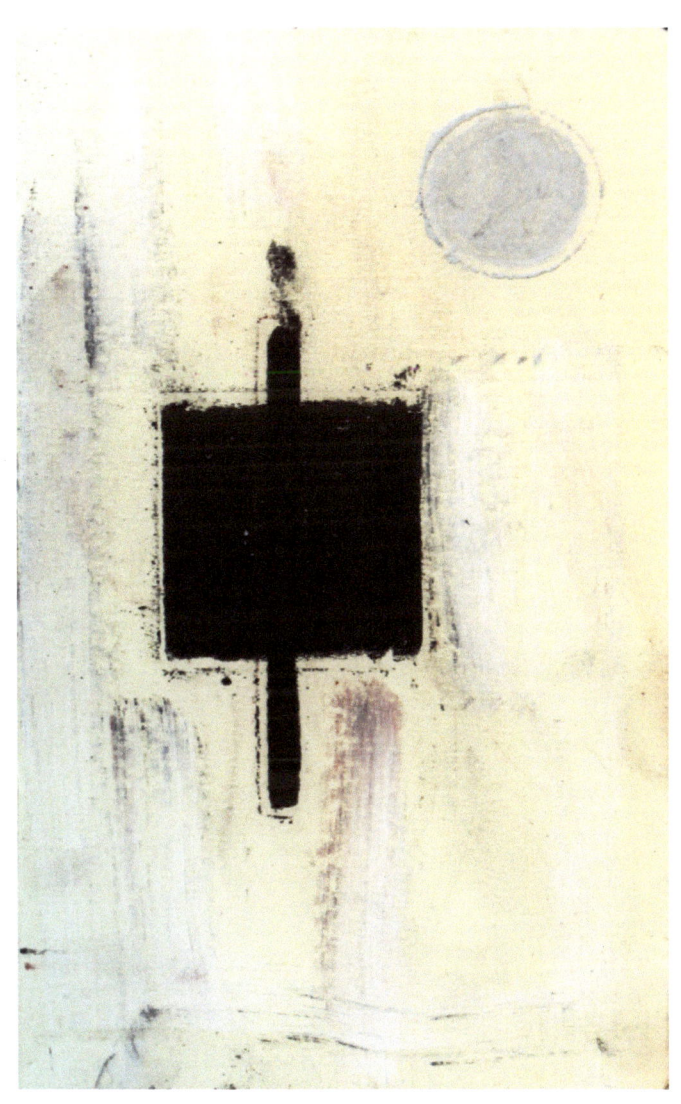

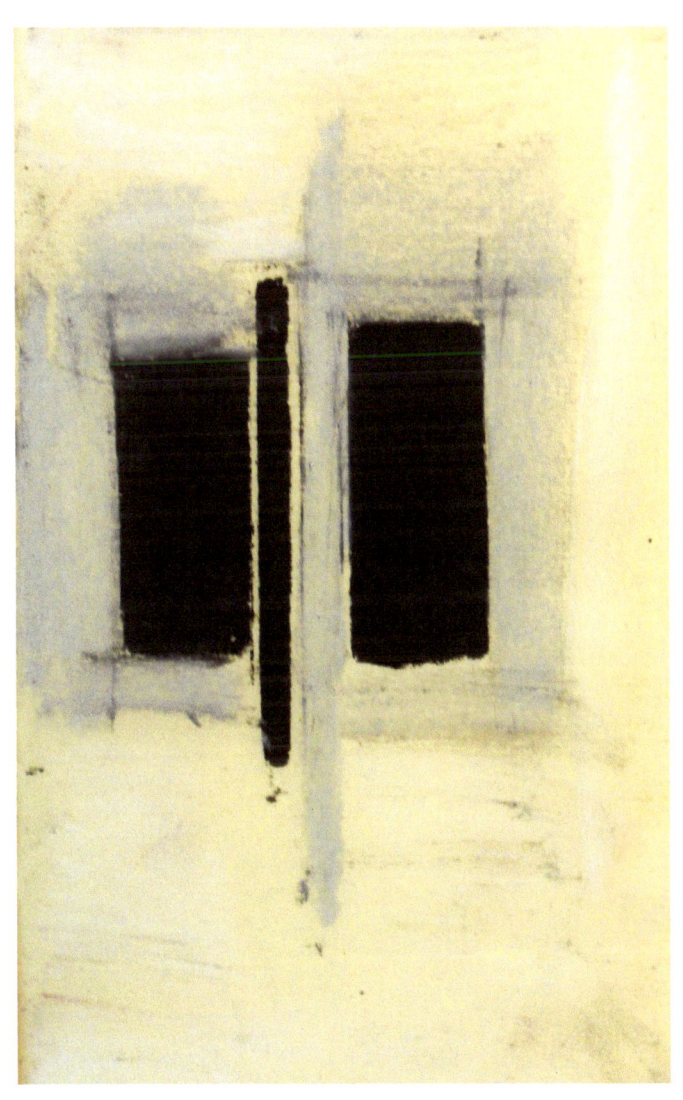

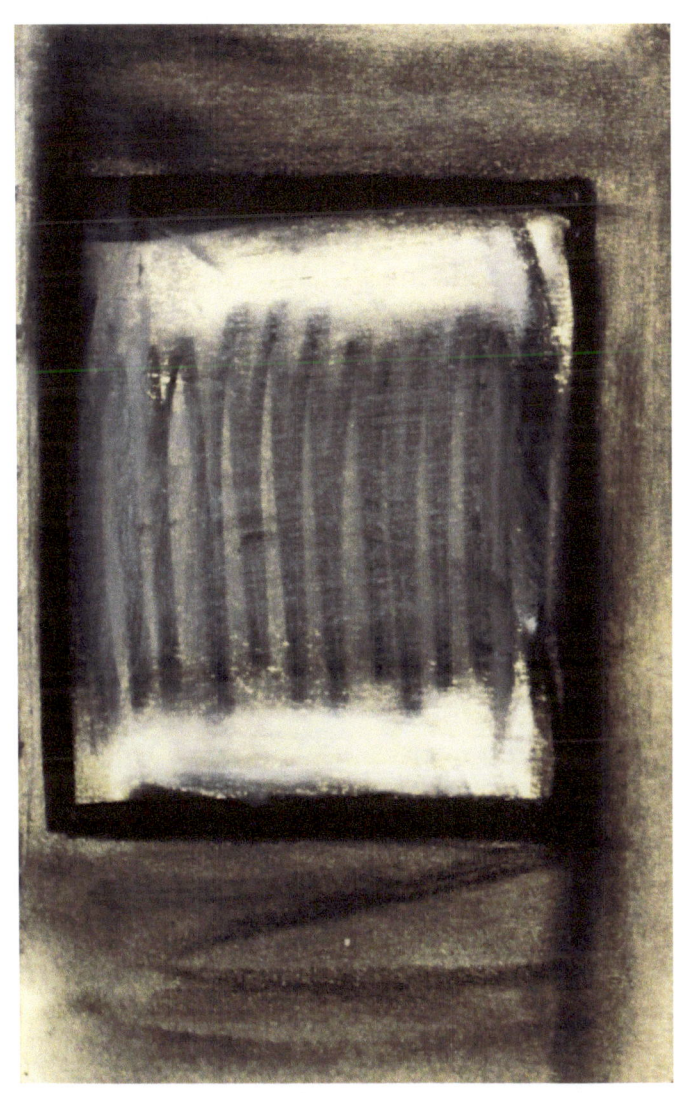

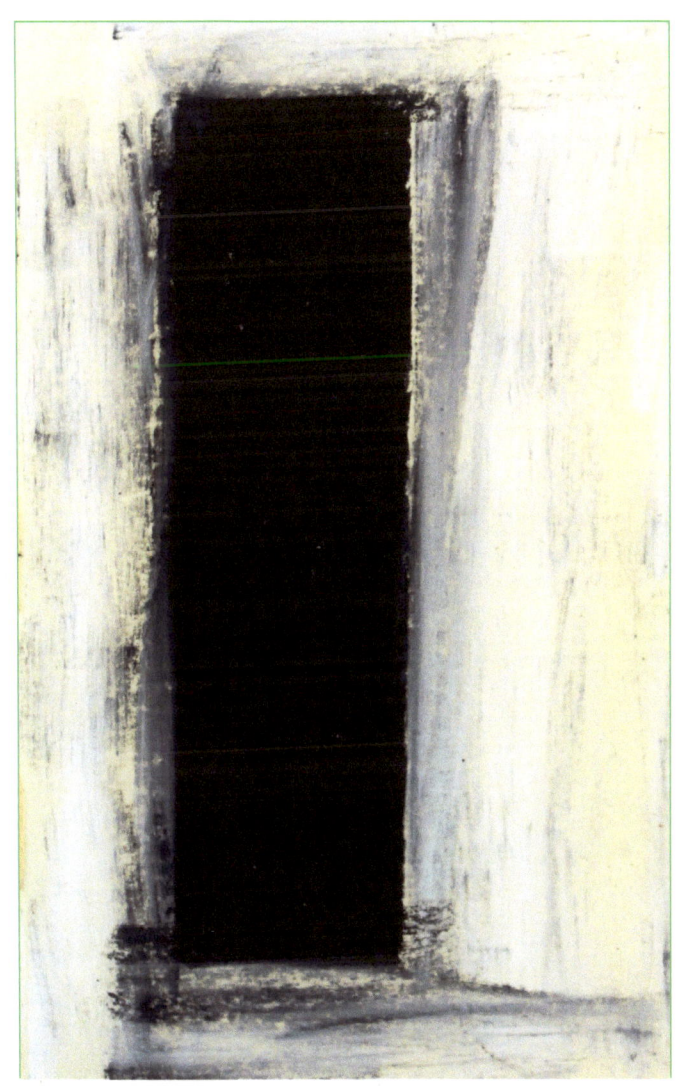

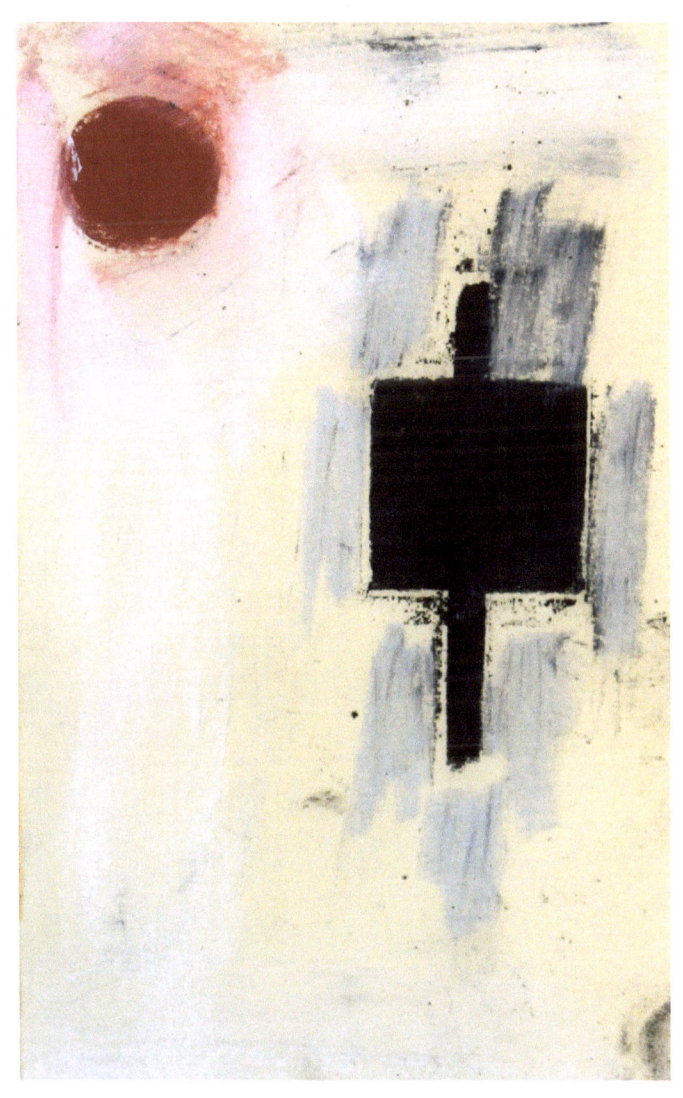

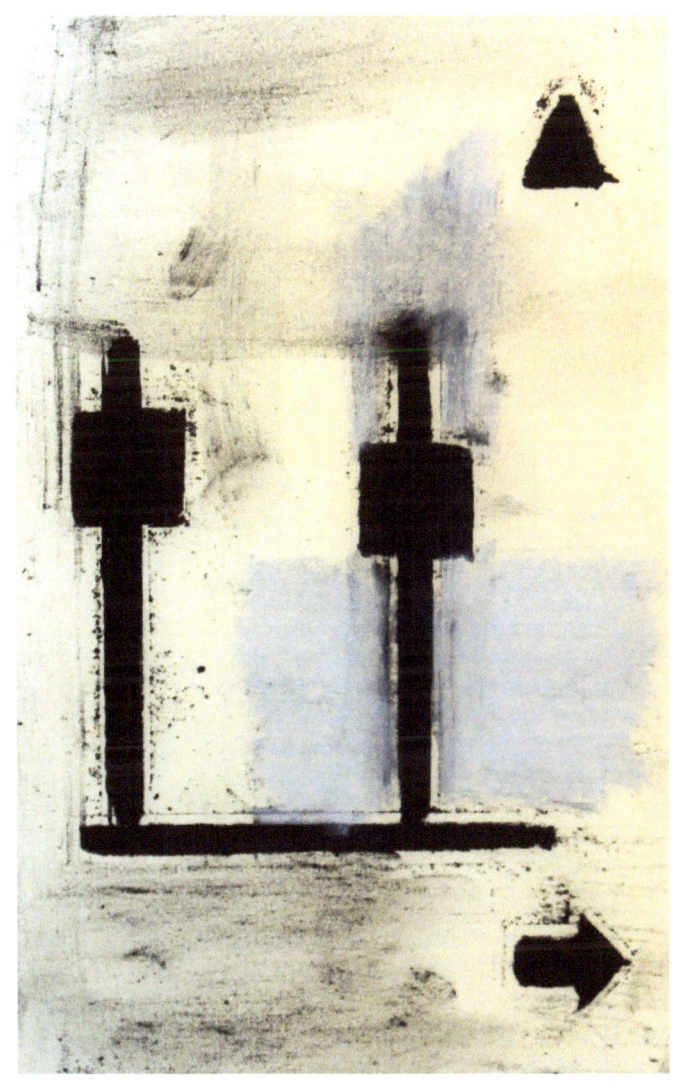

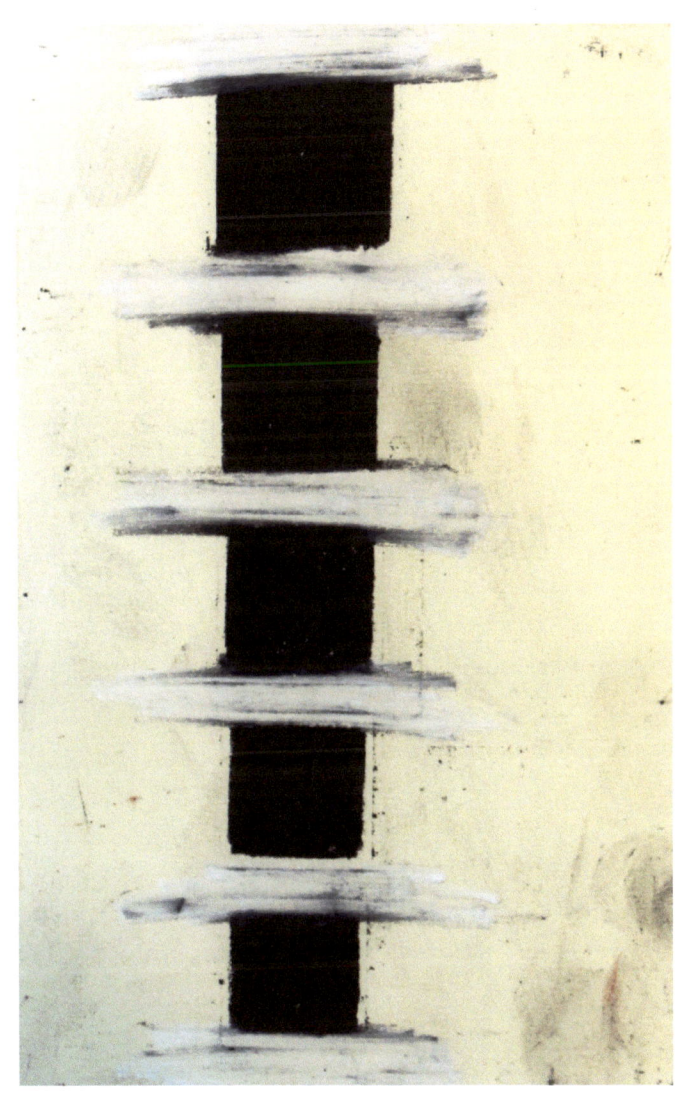

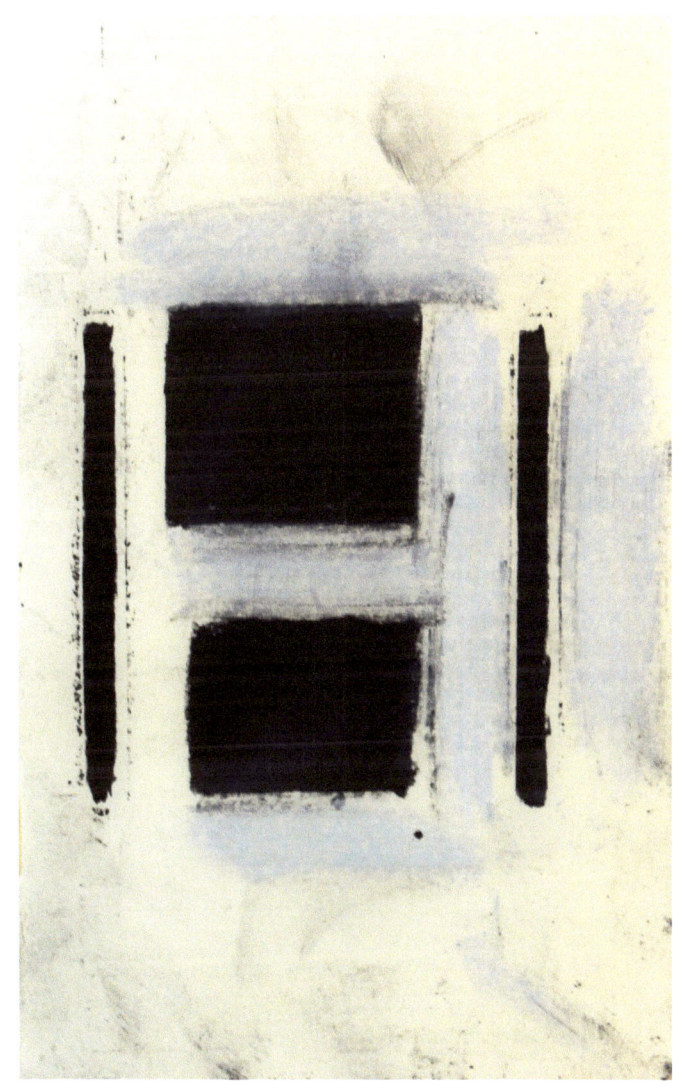

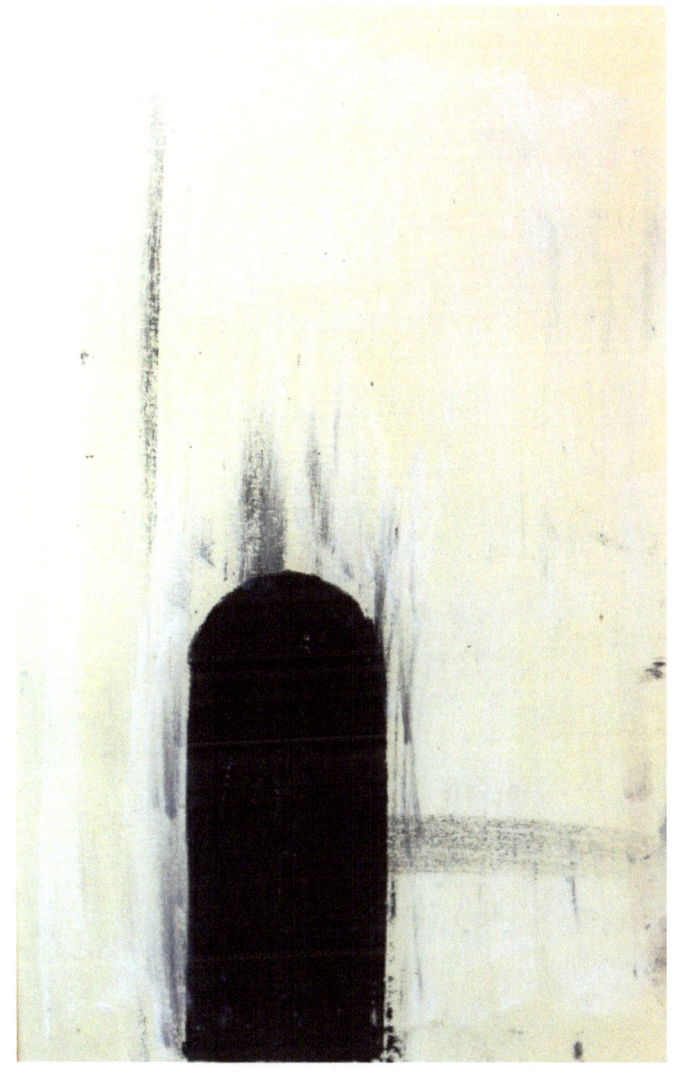

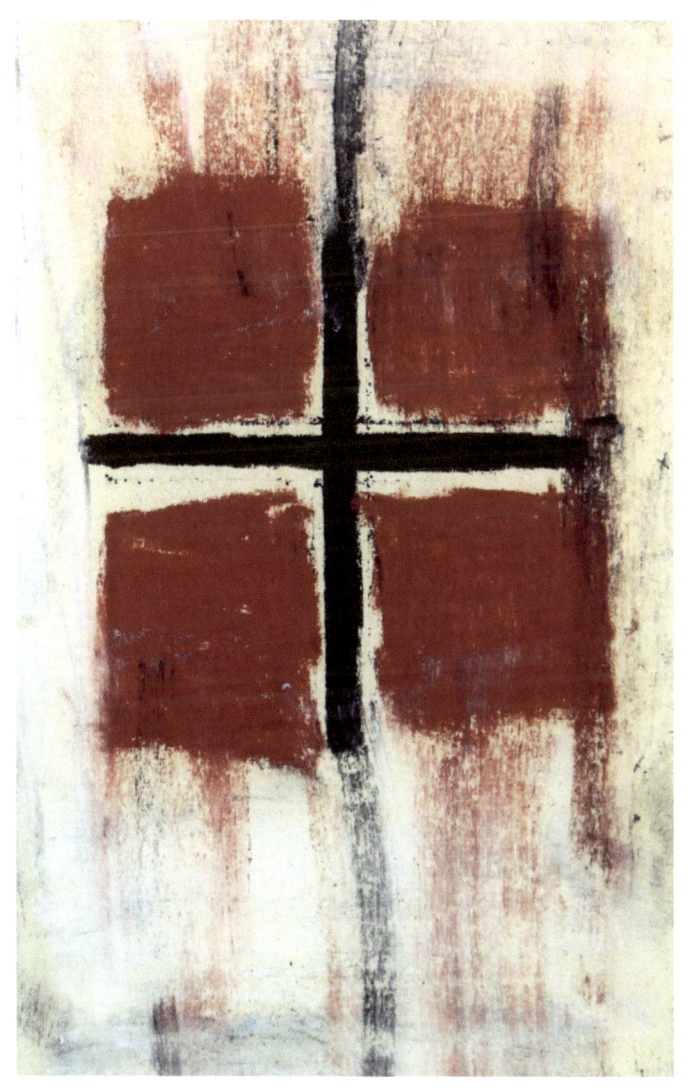

www.ingramcontent.com/pod-product-compliance
Lightning Source LLC
Chambersburg PA
CBHW040828180526
45159CB00001B/103